ENCHANTING ORIGAMI

Enchanted Meadow ORIGAMI

JOE FULLMAN

WINDMILL BOOKS

Published in 2021 by Windmill Books,
an Imprint of Rosen Publishing
29 East 21st Street, New York, NY 10010

Cataloging-in-Publication Data

Names: Fullman, Joe.
Title: Enchanted meadow origami / Joe Fullman.
Description: New York : Windmill Books, 2021. | Series: Enchanting origami | Includes glossary and index.
Identifiers: ISBN 9781499485370 (pbk.) | ISBN 9781499485394 (library bound) | ISBN 9781499485387 (6 pack) | ISBN 9781499485400 (ebook)
Subjects: LCSH: Origami--Juvenile literature. | Nature in art--Juvenile literature.
Classification: LCC TT872.5 F85 2021 | DDC 736'.982--dc23

Manufactured in the United States of America

CPSIA Compliance Information: Batch BS20WM: For Further Information contact Rosen Publishing, New York, New York at 1-800-237-9932

Contents

Introduction

Let's explore the wonderful world of enchanted origami. In this book, we'll venture out into the Magical Meadow, and help to fill it with pretty flowers, fluttering butterflies, and beautiful birds.

In traditional origami, the models are usually made from a single sheet of folded paper with no cutting or gluing involved. We've broken the rules here and there to make our models as magical as possible.

Ask an adult to help with any projects that need scissors and glue. Otherwise, all you need to get started is a square of paper and your fingers. If you haven't made origami models before, try some of the easy projects first. Now, let's get ready for some fantastic folding!

Getting Started

The paper used in origami is thin but strong, so that it can be folded many times. You can use ordinary scrap paper, as long as it's not too thick.

A lot of these origami models are made with the same folds and basic starting designs, known as "bases." This introduction explains some of the ones that will appear most, so it's a good idea to master these before you start. When making the projects, follow the key to find out what the lines and arrows mean. And always crease well!

Key

- Valley fold
- Mountain fold
- Step fold
- Direction to move paper
- Push/flatten
- Rotate by x degrees
- Cut with scissors
- Glue
- Turn paper over

Basic Folds

Valley Fold

To make a valley fold, fold the edges of the paper toward you, so that the crease is pointing down, like a valley.

Mountain Fold

To make a mountain fold, fold the edges of the paper away from you, so that the crease is pointing up, like a mountain.

Step Fold

A step fold is used to make a step or zigzag in the paper.

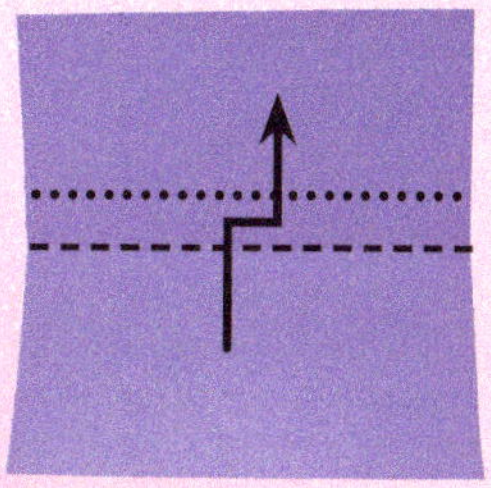

1

Valley fold the paper in half. Then make a mountain fold directly above the valley fold.

2

Push the mountain fold over the valley fold and press down flat.

3

You now have a step fold. You can also make it in reverse, with the mountain fold first.

Reverse Folds

Inside Reverse Fold

This is useful if you want to flatten part of an origami model. It's a good way to create legs and tails for your creatures.

1

Fold a piece of paper diagonally in half, as shown. Make a valley fold on one point and crease.

2

It's important to make sure that the paper is creased well. Run your finger over the crease two or three times.

3

Unfold, and then turn the crease you've just made into a mountain fold. Unfold, and open up the corner slightly.

4

Open up the paper a little more and then tuck the tip of the point inside. Close the paper. This is the view from the underside of the paper.

5

Flatten the paper. You now have an inside reverse fold.

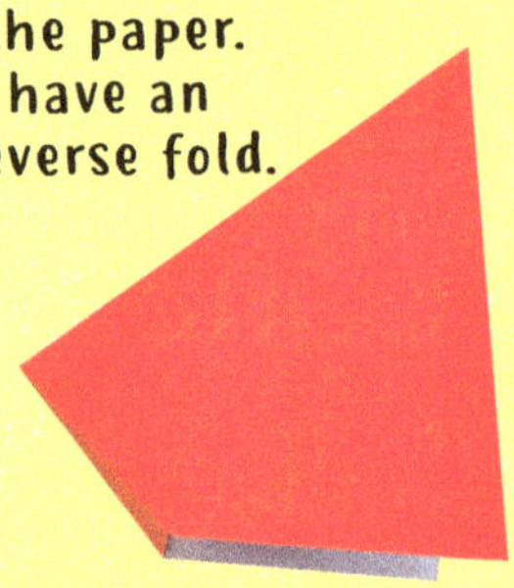

Outside Reverse Fold

This is great if you want to make part of your model stick out. It will come in handy for making heads and tails.

1

Fold a piece of paper diagonally in half, as shown. Make a valley fold on one point and crease.

2

It's important to make sure that the paper is creased well. Run your finger over the crease two or three times.

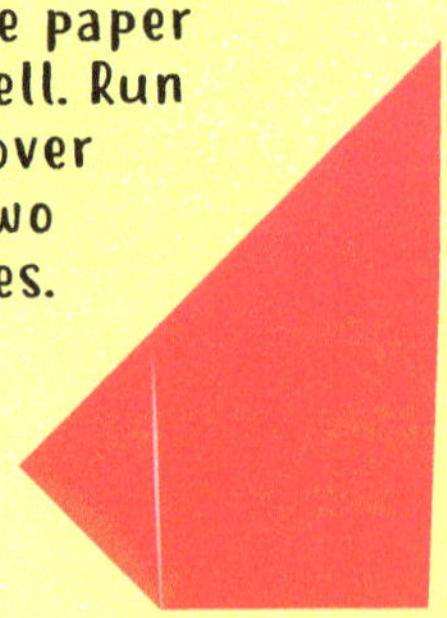

3

Unfold, and then turn the crease you've just made into a mountain fold. Unfold, and open up the corner slightly.

4

Open up the paper a little more and start to turn the corner inside out. Then close the paper when the fold begins to turn.

5

Flatten the paper. You now have an outside reverse fold.

Kite Base

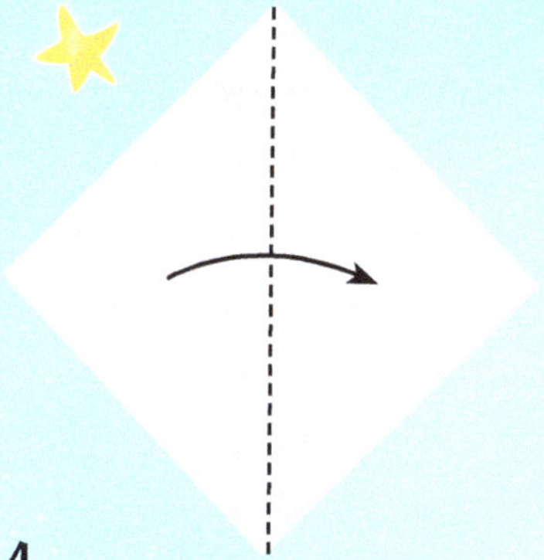

1

Place your paper like this. Valley fold it in half from left to right.

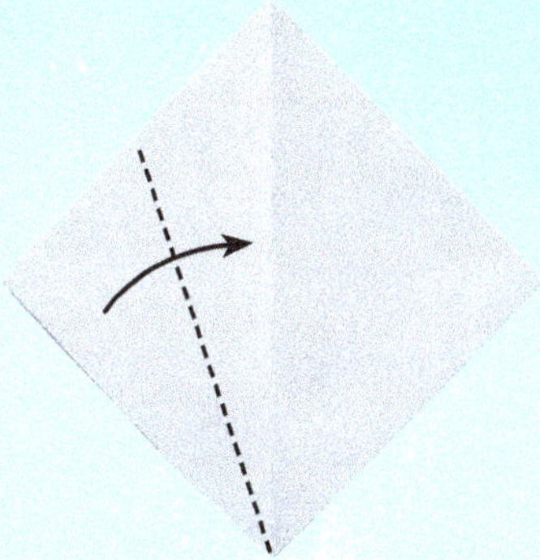

2

Valley fold the left-hand point over to the middle crease.

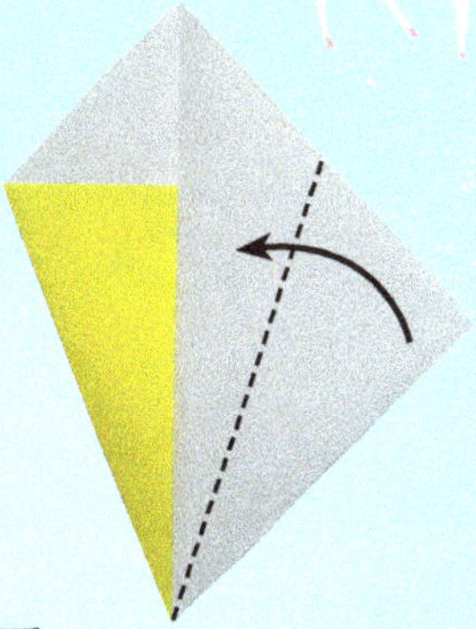

3

Repeat step 2 on the other side.

4

You now have a kite base.

Waterbomb Base

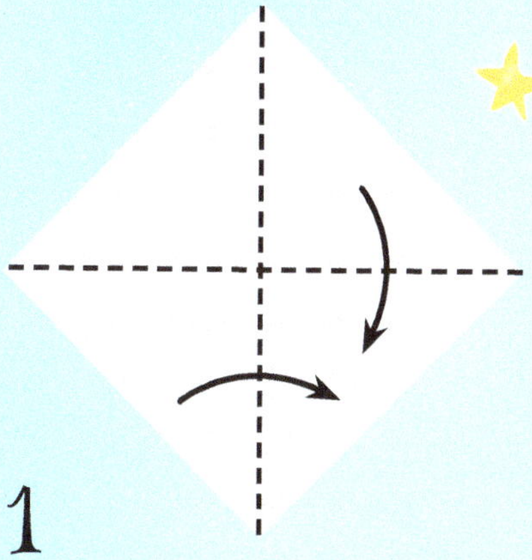

1

Start with a corner facing you. Valley fold from top to bottom and unfold. Then valley fold from left to right and unfold.

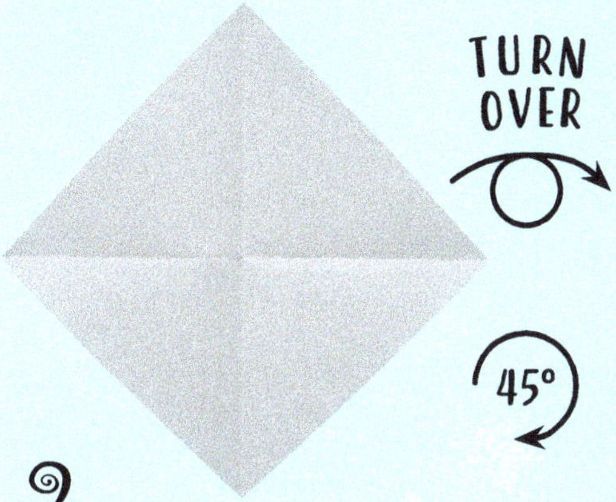

2

Turn your paper over and rotate it so that a straight edge is facing you.

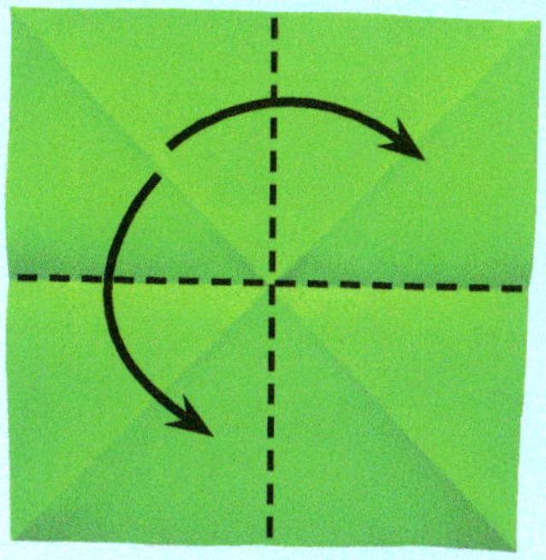

3

Valley fold from top to bottom and unfold. Then valley fold from left to right and unfold.

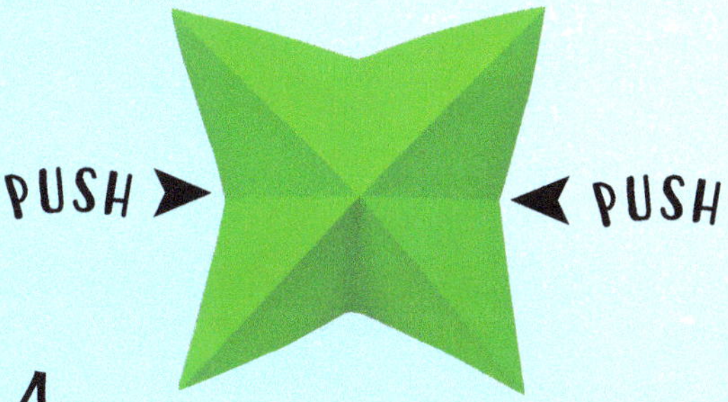

4

Push the sides of the paper together, so the middle point pops up.

5

Keep pushing the sides in, bringing the back and front sections together.

6

Flatten the paper down. You now have a waterbomb base.

Magic Flower

Let's start with some pretty flowers. You'll need glue and two pieces of paper for this project. One sheet of paper should be green, to make the stem.

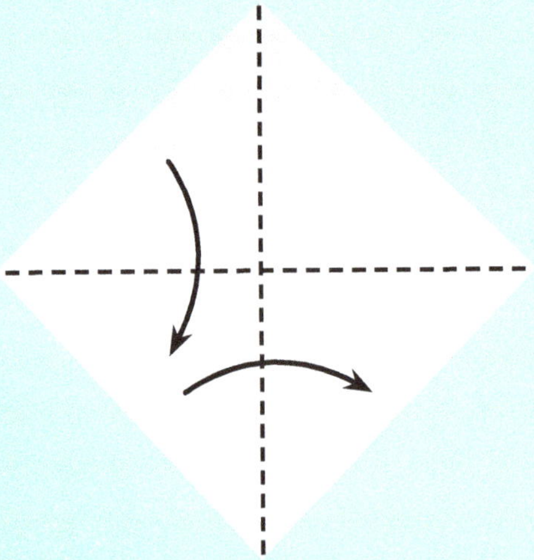

1

Start by making the flower. Place your non-green paper like this, white side up with a corner facing you. Valley fold in half from left to right, and unfold. Then valley fold in half from top to bottom, and unfold.

2

Turn the paper over from left to right.

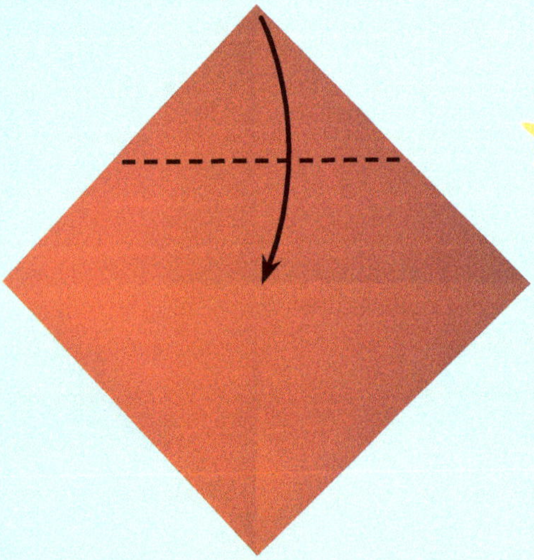

3

Valley fold the top corner down to the central crease.

4

Valley fold the top edge down to the central crease.

Easy

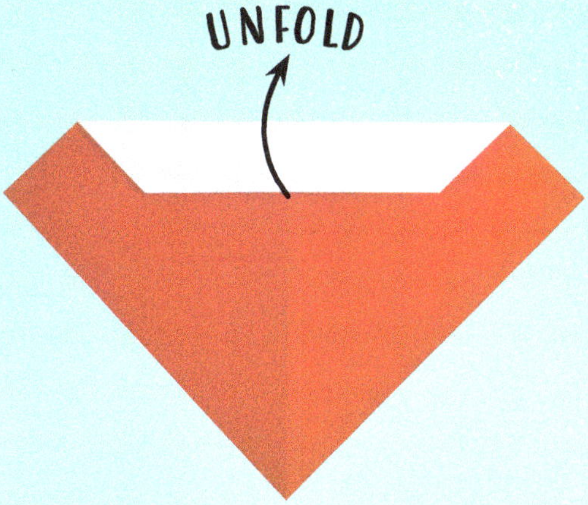

5

Unfold the folds you made in steps 3 and 4.

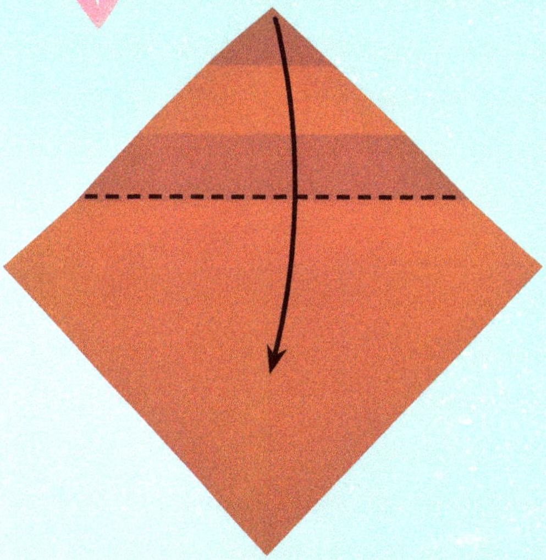

6

Valley fold the top corner down again along the line of the third crease line from the top.

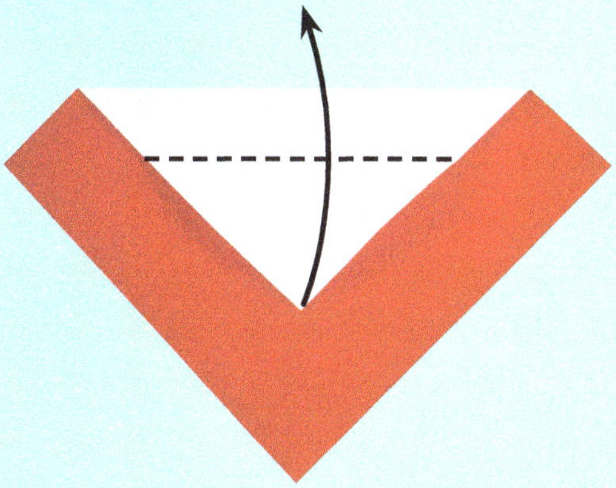

7

Valley fold the point back up again as shown, now using the first crease line from the top.

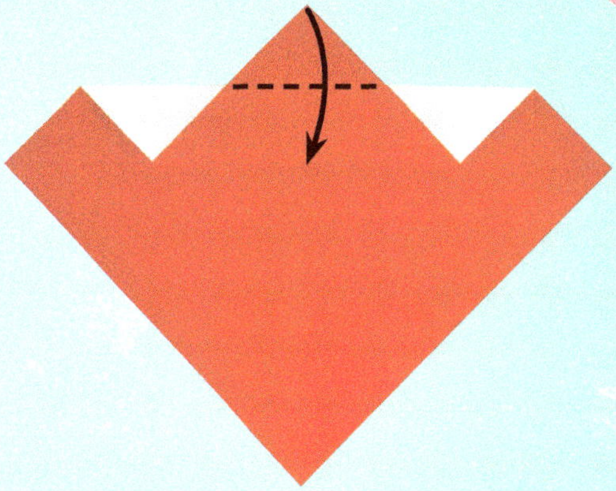

8

Valley fold the point down again using the remaining crease line.

9

Mountain fold the left, right, and bottom points, as shown.

10

Your flower is ready. Put it to one side and get the green piece of paper so you can make the stalk.

11

Place your paper like this, white side up with a corner facing you. Fold in half from left to right, then unfold.

12

Fold the paper in half from bottom to top.

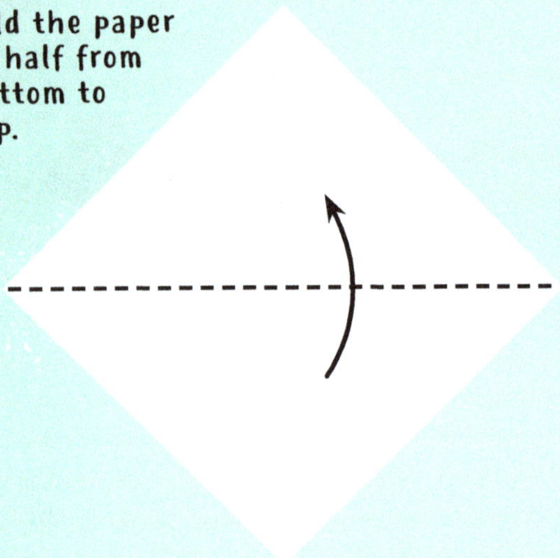

13

Fold the top right edge over to the central crease.

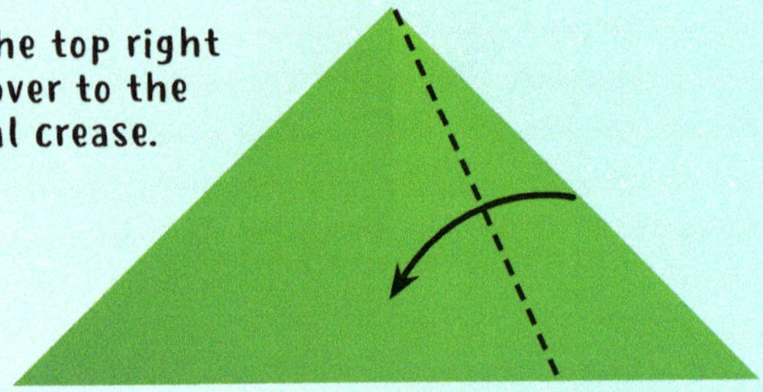

14

Repeat step 13 on the left-hand side.

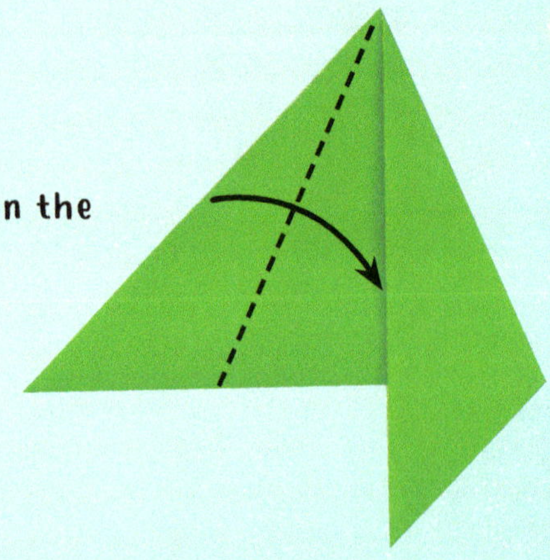

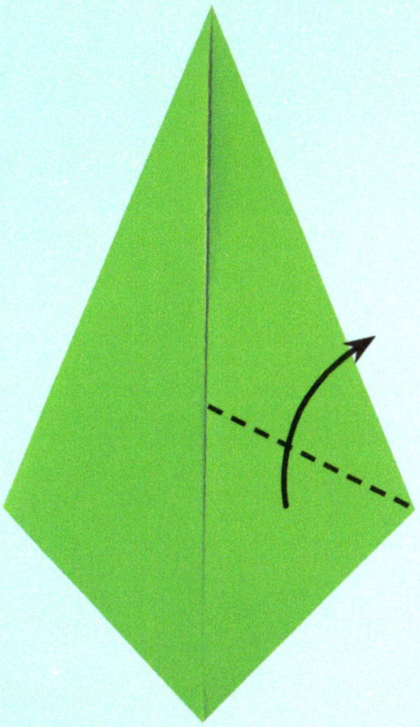

15
Valley fold the bottom right point up at an angle, as shown.

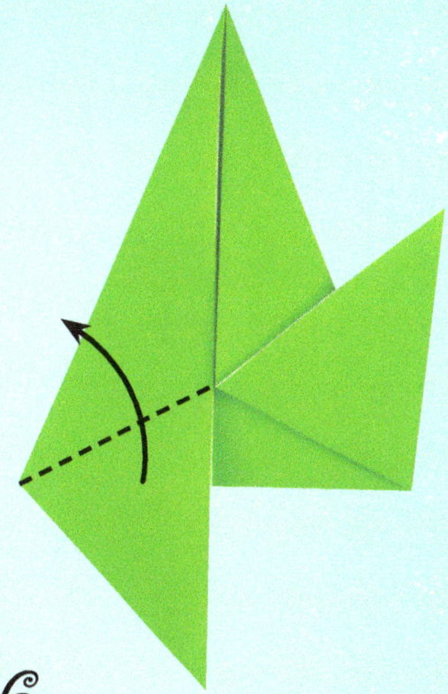

16
Repeat step 15 on the left-hand side.

17
Your paper should look like this. Get your flower and carefully attach it to the top of your stalk with glue.

18
That's one flower done. Why don't you make more for your enchanted meadow?

Cute Cactus

Follow these steps to create your own spiky cactus for the Magical Meadow to go alongside your flowers. You'll need a green piece of paper.

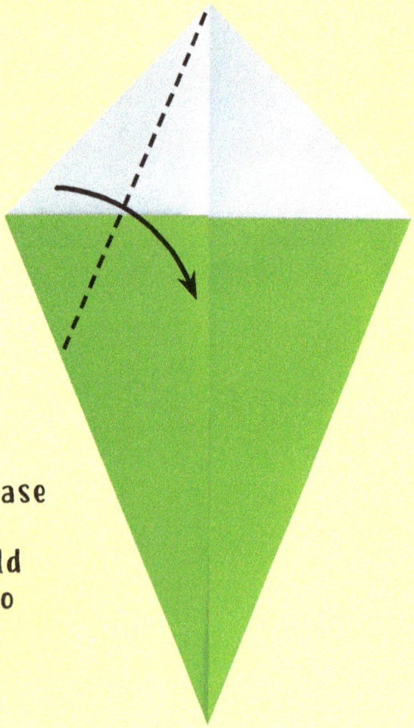

1

Start with a kite base (see page 7) placed like this. Valley fold the top left edge to the central crease.

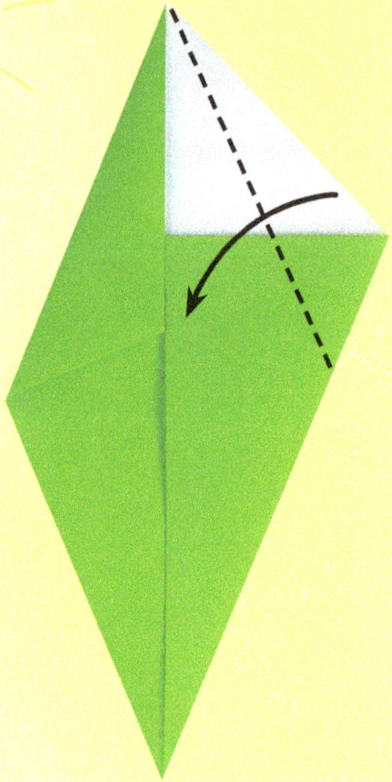

2

Repeat step 1 on the right-hand side.

3

Open up the fold you made in step 1.

4

Pull the middle point down along the central line, so that it forms a triangle-shaped flap.

Medium

5

Flatten the paper down.

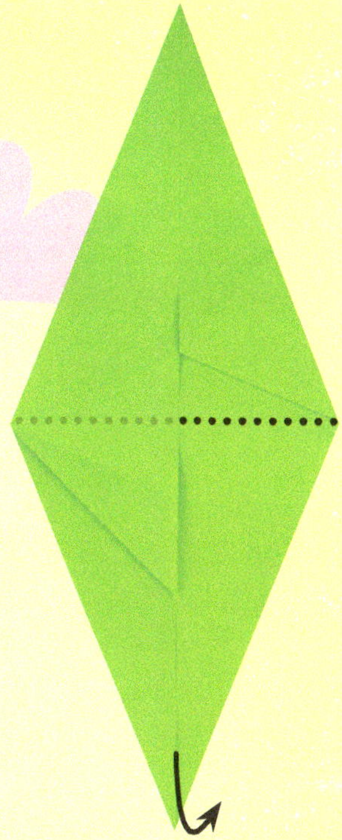

6

Mountain fold the paper in half from bottom to top behind the flap you made in steps 3 to 5, so the flap is left pointing downward.

7

Your paper should look like this. Turn it over from left to right.

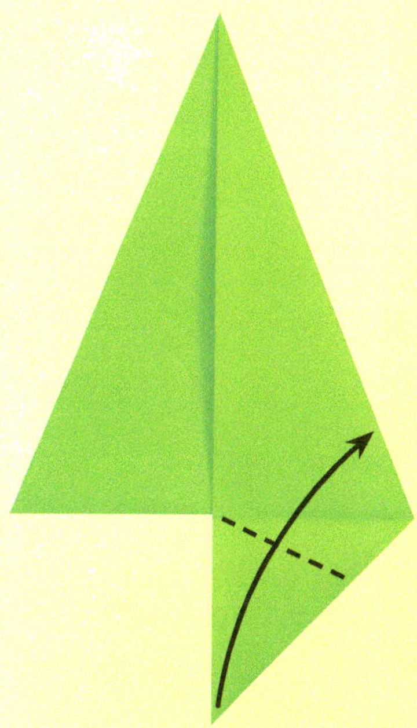

8

Valley fold the bottom point up and to the right at an angle so it touches the right-hand edge.

9

Turn the paper over from left to right.

10

Valley fold the right-hand point across at an angle, as shown.

11

Fold the top point of the upper layer down and to the right, so part of it goes over the flap you made in step 10.

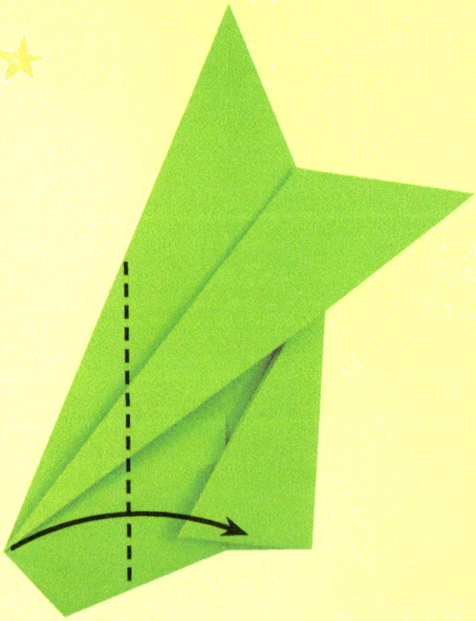

12

Valley fold the bottom left point across so it's roughly in line with the fold you made in step 10. This should reveal the triangle-shaped flap behind it.

Medium

13

As you fold, a small flap should form at the bottom of the paper between the new flap and the smaller triangle-shaped flap. Flatten this down.

14

Make four small valley folds, as shown.

15

Make a small valley fold at the bottom, as shown, then turn the paper over from left to right.

16

Your cactus is ready to get some sun. They like it hot.

Toadstool Seat

This origami toadstool will make a comfortable seat for a fairy or a unicorn foal. Choose brightly patterned paper to make your toadstool extra magical.

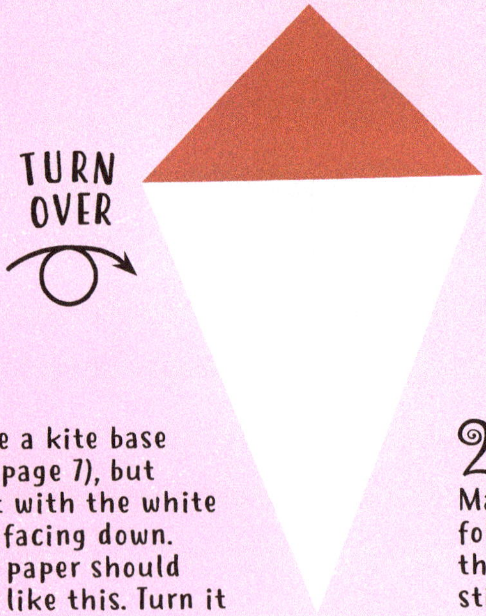

1

Make a kite base (see page 7), but start with the white side facing down. Your paper should look like this. Turn it over from left to right.

2

Make a mountain fold, as shown, so the bottom point sticks out above the top point.

3

Unfold the fold you made in step 2.

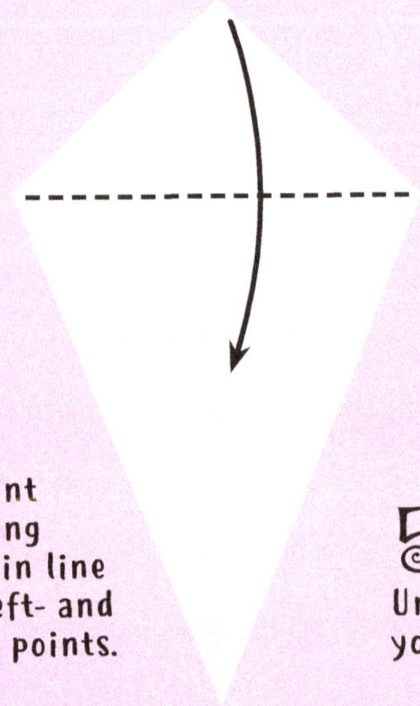

4

Valley fold the top point down, making the crease in line with the left- and right-hand points.

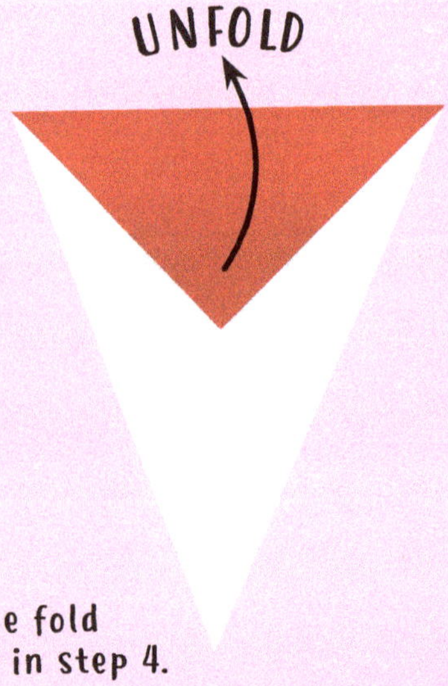

5

Unfold the fold you made in step 4.

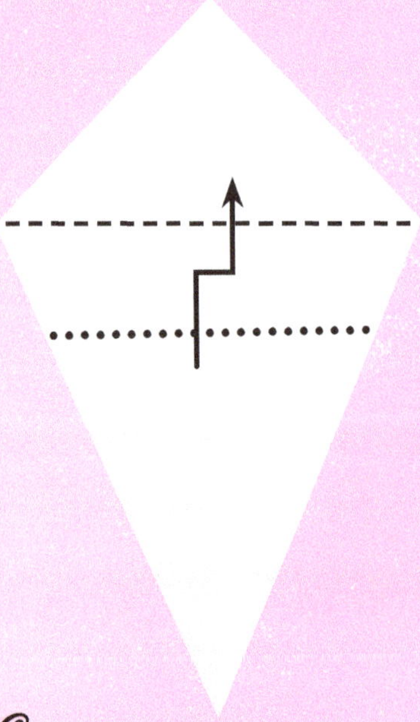

6

Turn the creases you made in steps 2 and 4 into a step fold.

Medium

7

Open up the right-hand side and bring the top right point down and to the left.

8

Flatten your paper down.

9

Your paper should look like this. Repeat steps 7 and 8 on the left-hand side.

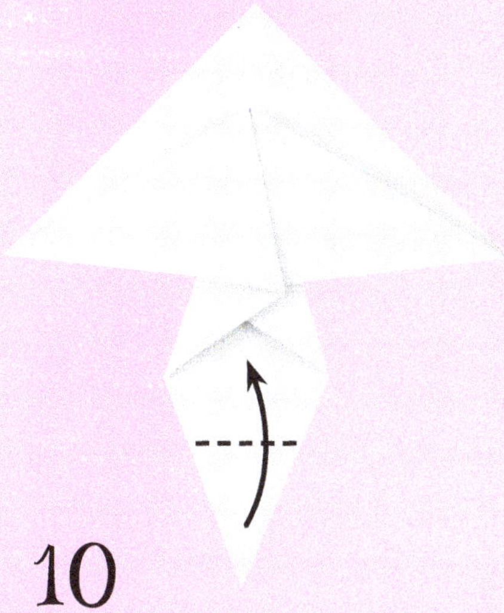

10

Valley fold the bottom point.

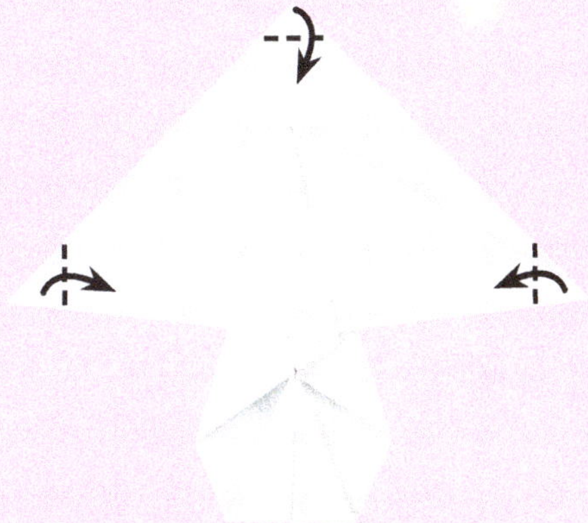

11

Make three small valley folds, as shown.

12

Turn the paper over from left to right.

13

And there's your toadstool. Add some decorations to make it as welcoming as possible.

Fluttering Butterfly

What's this fluttering across the Magical Meadow? It's a beautiful butterfly. Use the prettiest paper you can find for this project.

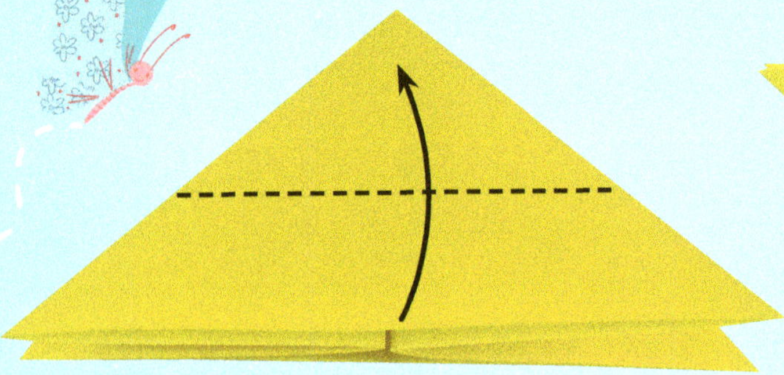

1

Start by making a waterbomb base (see page 7), then valley fold the bottom edge to just below the top point, as shown.

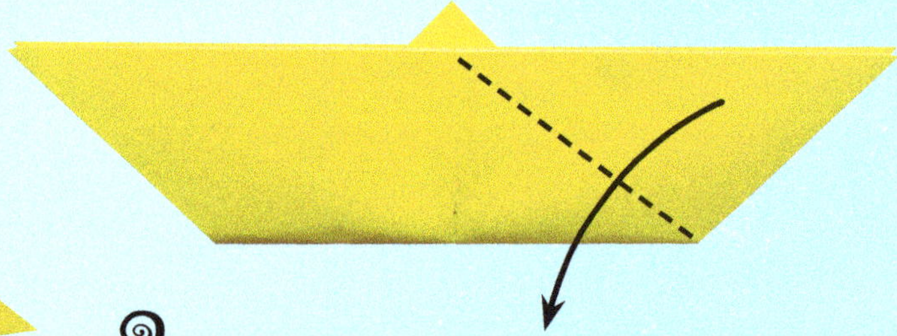

2

Valley fold the top right point of the upper layer down and to the left.

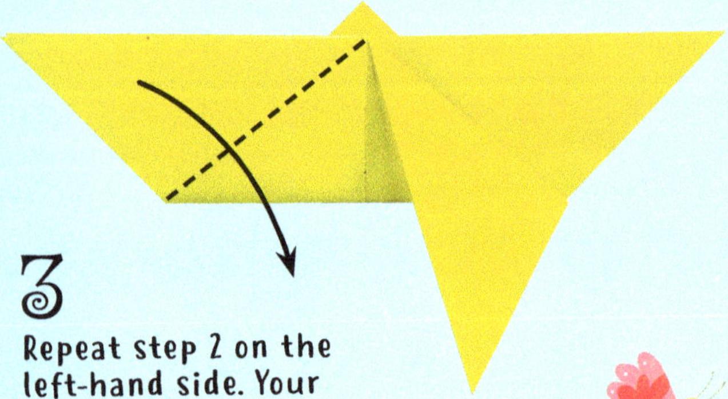

3

Repeat step 2 on the left-hand side. Your butterfly's wings are now complete.

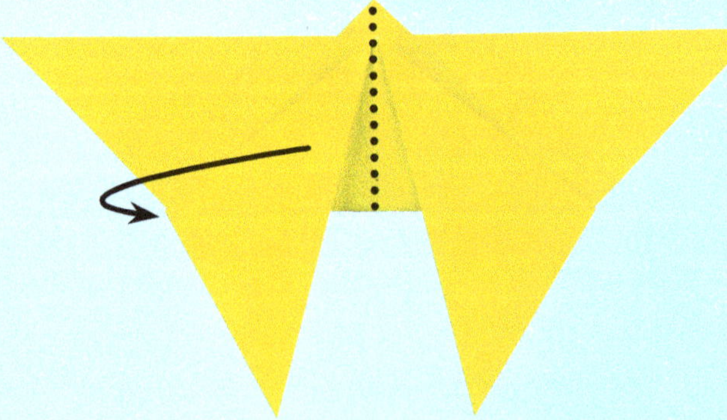

4

Mountain fold the paper in half from left to right.

Easy

5

Make a mountain fold as shown, folding through all the layers. You'll need to press hard!

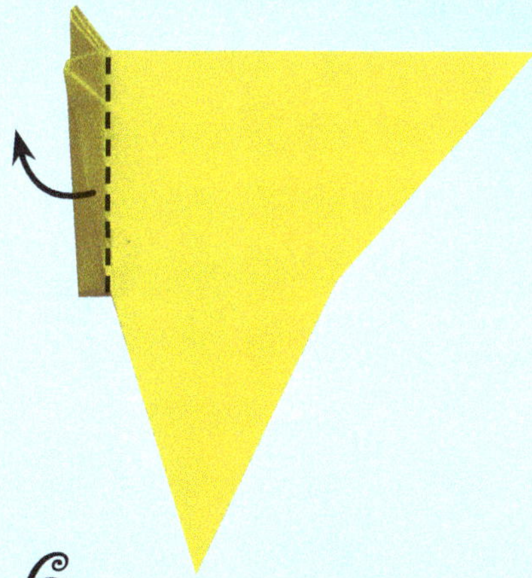

6

Fold it the other way, so it's also a valley fold, then unfold.

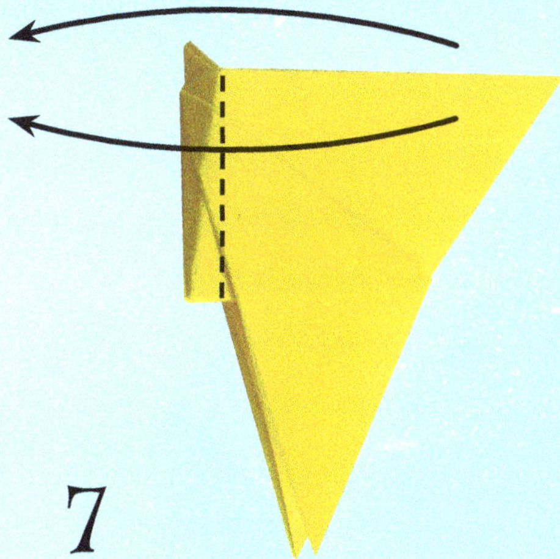

7

Fold both wings to the left, on either side of the fold lines you made in steps 5 and 6.

8

Your paper should look like this. Unfold the upper wing.

9

Your beautiful butterfly is ready. Add some patterns to its wings.

Beautiful Bird

This bird is a frequent visitor to the Magical Meadow, fluttering over the flowers.

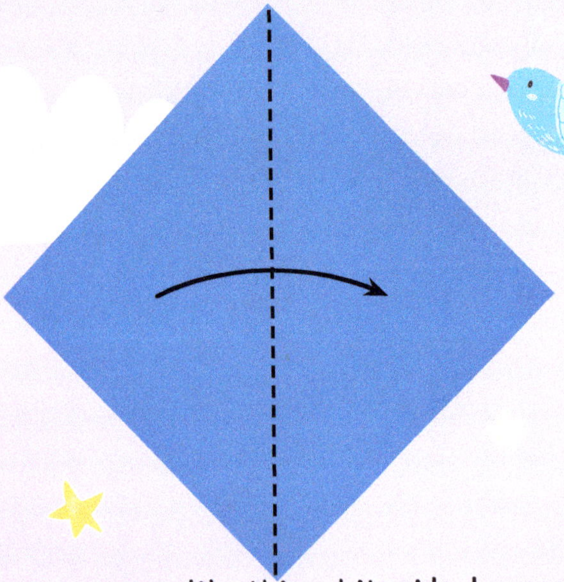

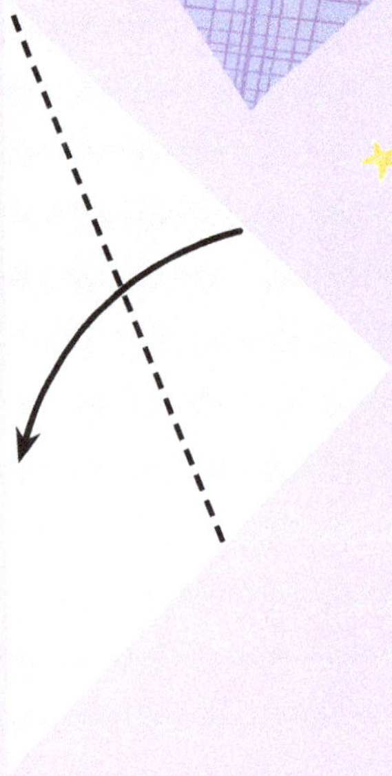

1

Place your paper like this, white side down with a corner facing you. Valley fold it in half from left to right.

2

Valley fold the top right edge of the upper layer over to the central crease.

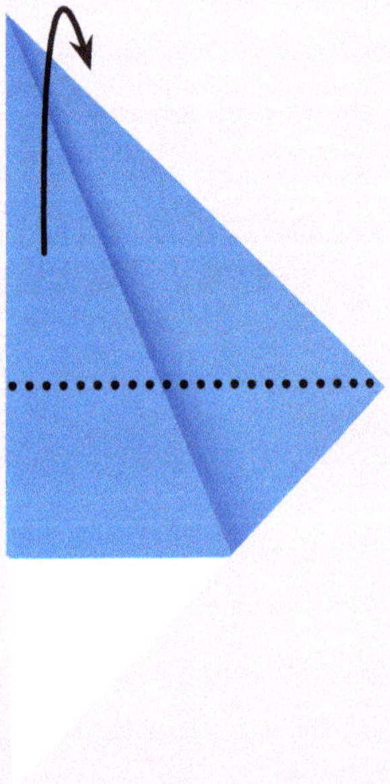

3

Mountain fold the paper in half from top to bottom.

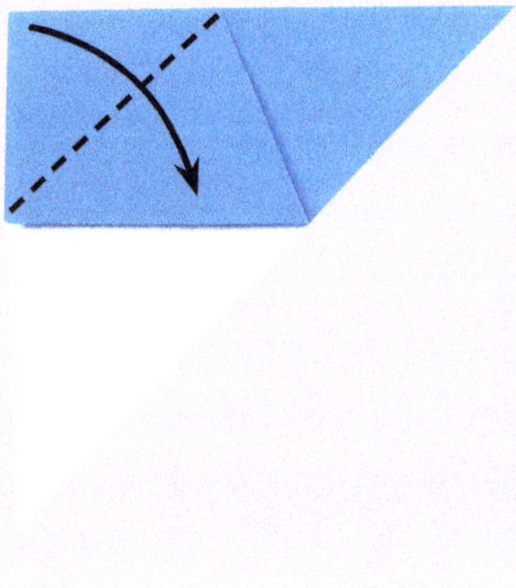

4

Valley fold the top left-hand corner, but don't flatten it right down.

5

Unfold the fold you made in step 4.

Medium

6

Open out the paper on the left side. Pull the middle left point of the upper layer up toward the top, keeping it in line with the left-hand edge.

7

As you pull, the middle right point should start lifting up and coming over to the left, forming a shape like a bird's mouth. Flatten the paper down.

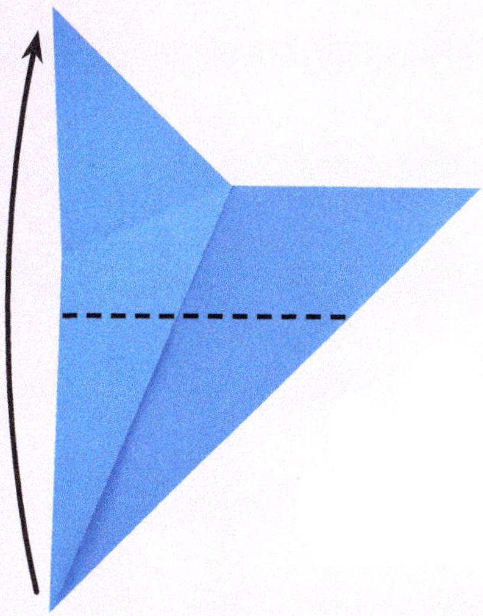

8

Your paper should look like this. Valley fold the bottom point of the upper layer so it lines up with the top left point.

9

Mountain fold the bottom point so it lines up with the top point.

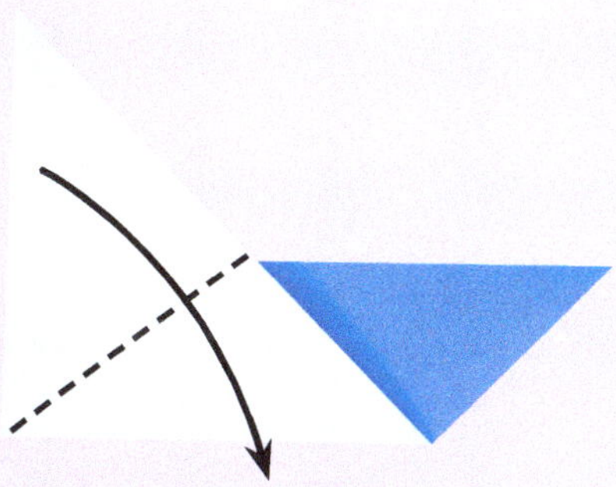

10

Make a diagonal valley fold in the upper layer, as shown, to form the first wing.

11

Turn the paper over, repeat step 10 on the other side, then turn the paper back over again. Your paper should look like this.

12

Make a valley fold on the right-hand side, then unfold.

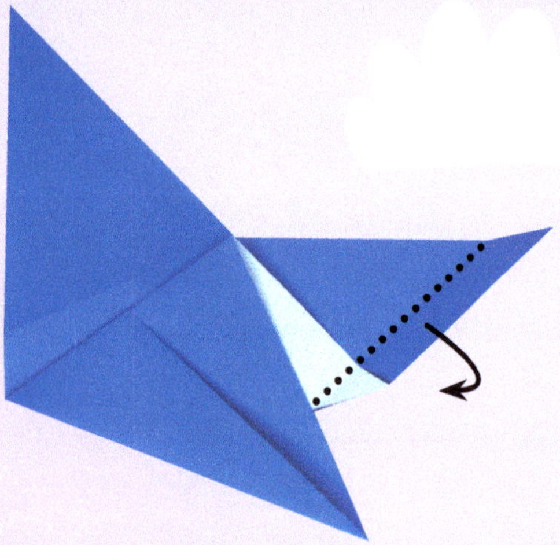

13

Fold it the other way, so it's also a mountain fold, then turn it into an outside reverse fold (see page 6).

14

Make a mountain fold on the top, as shown.

15

Unfold the fold you made in step 14.

Medium

16

Fold it the other way, so it's also a valley fold, then turn it into an inside reverse fold (see page 6).

17

Mountain fold the bottom left point of the upper layer.

18

Make a matching fold on the other side.

19

Your paper should look like this. Carefully pull the wings apart and your bird should be able to stand up on its wings.

20

You could use different types of paper to create a whole flock of birds for your meadow.

Glossary

CREASE A line made by a fold.

DIAGONAL A line in a sloping direction, from one corner to another.

KITE BASE A starting shape that looks like a kite.

MOUNTAIN FOLD A fold where the crease points up, like a mountain.

STEP FOLD A fold that creates a zigzag, or step, in the paper.

VALLEY FOLD A fold where the crease points away from you, like a valley.

Further Information

James, Elizabeth. *Easy Origami for Children.* Twickenham, UK: Kyle Craig Publishing, 2017.

Montroll, John. *Dragons and Other Fantastic Creatures in Origami.* Mineola, NY: Dover Publications, 2014.

Stephen, Ella. *Origami for Kids.* Independently published, 2019.

Top That Publishing. *Fold Your Own Fantastic Fairytale Unicorns.* Woodbridge, UK: Top That Publishing, 2019.

Index